ARIZONA
HIGHWAYS BOOK

Selected writings of
Raymond Carlson
Editor
Arizona Highways magazine
1938-1971

Photography by
Arizona Highways
Contributors

Remembering Raymond...

$\mathcal{R}$ emembering Raymond...We who were fortunate to know him—and that included millions of readers of *Arizona Highways Magazine* over some four decades—recognized in Raymond Carlson a Renaissance man. His head had been schooled in disciplined English, yet his heart was forever fetching him off into unabashed lyric and unashamed sermon. Of Raymond we all could testify:

> *More is a man of angel's wit and singular learning. I know not his fellow. For where is the man of that gentleness, lowliness and affability? And as time requireth, a man of marvelous mirth and pastimes; and sometimes of as sad a gravity; a man for all seasons.*

Raymond wrote well about the seasonal cycles of sun and storm, frost and bloom so manifest in the West. "Arizona is geology by day and astronomy by night," he once observed, and, "We have often been asked by many well-meaning and truly interested and serious askers what we feel is the most delightful month in Arizona. Our answer is a simple one but one that leaves us slightly out of breath. It is this: *januaryfebruarymarchaprilmayjunejulyaugust-septemberoctobernovemberdecember.*" In an editorial he confessed that he considered his mission of chronicling the seasons of the Great Southwest as "more than a job—it is a crusade."

While reflecting upon such a devoted spirit and wondering how he might be eulogized, it crossed my mind that Alan Lerner in *Camelot* already summed up Raymond Carlson's love affair with his special corner of Earth:

> *If ever I would leave you,*
> *It wouldn't be in summer...*
> *Your hair streaked with sunlight,*
> *Your lips red as flame,*
> *Your face with a lustre,*
> *That puts gold to shame!*

Miner's son, University of Arizona alumnus, Phi Beta Kappa graduate of Stanford University, Depression-era busboy, small-town newsman, Carlson became the sixth editor of *Arizona Highways* in 1938.

He inherited a 3500-circulation, state-sponsored periodical which largely had consisted of road bulletins, governmental reports, and industry advertisements. Carlson discontinued the ads and in full-color photography launched his crusade "to bring you in word and picture the story of our state, yesterday, today and tomorrow; to guide your pleasant journey through this smiling land of time enough and room enough to tell you of the unhurried life therein; to point your way to the distant places throughout our Great Southwest, which add to your travels the spice of adventure and discovery; and, to share with you our pride in our own corner of America, the deep West, so rich in scenic enchantment, so colorful, so memorable it is beyond compare."

But if I'd ever leave you,
It couldn't be in autumn...
I've seen how you sparkle,
When fall nips the air.
I know you in autumn.
And I must be there.

But for a two-year stint in the Pacific with the Sixth Infantry Division (he won a Bronze Star for valor in combat in New Guinea), Raymond guided the improbable growth of *Highways* circulation to 100,000...300,000...and for some special issues...beyond 1 million. Through it all he lavished lilting essays upon the greater region of Arizona and its surroundings. He splurged an entire edition on Mexican travel and lifeways, and another on the splendors of the neighboring state of Utah. His editorials were nothing less than love letters to his homeland—which he often personified as a woman of breathtaking beauty.

It amounted to radical, early-day environmentalism. Much more than a travel journal, *Highways* unquestionably encouraged the preservation of national refuges, state and local parks, and scenic highway vistas. Of numerous awards, perhaps the most satisfying to Raymond was the Department of the Interior Conservation Service Award. The citation from Secretary of the Interior Stewart L. Udall in 1966 commented: "Your approach to conservation

has not been to view with alarm, but rather to view with admiration, and you have succeeded in transmitting this feeling to your readers. By means of your magnificent photographs and carefully selected articles, you have stimulated a greater appreciation of Nature in the minds and hearts of readers in many parts of the world to which your magazine is sent. In this gentle and pleasant way, you have done much to create a widespread desire to preserve the things that should be preserved."

And could I leave you
Running merrily through the snow?
Or on a wintry evening
When you catch the fire's glow?

Raymond's enthusiasm, good nature, stylish intellect, and unerring editorial instinct attracted authors, artists, and photographers of first rank. Ansel Adams, Esther Henderson, and Josef Muench volunteered their imaginative visions for Raymond's pioneering pages of color printing. Ernie Pyle, J. Frank Dobie, Mary Kidder Rak, and Donald Culross Peattie wrote for him. The artistry of Maynard Dixon, N. C. Wyeth, Ted DeGrazia, and Nicolai Fechin formed folios for Raymond's own seasonal prose poems. In sum of parts, *Highways* brought together the right people with relevant ideas about an emerging region at exactly the right time.

In 1971 because of diminished health, Raymond retired. He remained on the masthead as Editor Emeritus, but his energies steadily declined. He spent his final months in a nursing home, and in January, 1983, he did indeed—despite his promises—depart the Southwestern world he loved so fervently.

This book is dedicated to him. His words as they are excerpted from his magazine editorials for reprinting in this book suggest that he kept his promise to us after all.

Knowing how in spring I'm
Bewitched by you so?
Oh, no! Not in springtime!
Summer, winter or fall!
No, never could I leave you
At all!

—Don Dedera

Summer Wears a Green Gown...

If ever I would leave you,
It wouldn't be in summer...

Black River reflections in the White Mountains.
David Muench

*S*ummer...She wears that old, old look. Paris shears have not altered the hem of her skirt nor changed the line of her bodice. Bespectacled little chemists, stirring the brew in their odorous dye pots, have concocted no outlandish colors for her to go swishing about in. Slick and glossy fashion editors of slick and glossy fashion magazines seldom call on her for an interview. She carries no appointments for sittings before high-powered cameras operated by high-powered young men. She's just as plain as can be. Her plainness is the essence of poise and dignity.

She wears a green gown, and it is mighty becoming. It isn't a monotonous green, mind you. It is the gray green of the saguaro, the silvery green of ripening grain, the dark green of the pine, the bright green of the sycamore, the light green of weeds on a canal bank, the green of olives with a faintly bluish cast, the just-right green of new mown grass.

She's composed, serene and smiling, and carries herself as if she were somebody, which, in truth, she is. She's so cool and calm in her lovely green gown, and she has the loveliest name. Her name is Summer.

(Left) Butterfly in the Coconino National Forest. George McCullough

(Right) Summer in the White Mountains. Jerry Jacka

(Left, below) Rocky Mountain mule deer in the Kaibab National Forest. James Tallon

(Below) Nature's garden in the Apache-Sitgreaves National Forest. Jerry Jacka

Tranquillity

There are many definitions of tranquillity. It might be described in one way as one being at peace in Nature's world around and about. It comes to the sailor on the placid seas; it comes to the mountain man, surrounded by the green and serene forests. It comes to the dweller in the desert land.

Here is distance and stillness and peace... here only the marks of the Sun, of the fitful wind, of the changing seasons which represent the errant notations of time's dreamy passing.

When you live in a big land, but not over-populated, just a few minutes drive and there you are; in the tranquil world of Nature. If you make your peace with that world you have attained man's most desirable state of being: tranquillity...

The lonely acres may be the answer to the yearning that is deep within all of us that sometime, someplace we may be where Nature's handiwork is unaltered and our companions are the Sun, the wind, and the eternal skies with their depths of blue at day and their star-filled radiance at night.

The desert is a place for contemplation and reverie. One might ponder the inscrutable ways of the Creator that provide a brave living for the flora and fauna of the desert that live and survive and even flourish under conditions that could be described, even generously, as harsh...

Here the boundary of one's world is the shimmering horizon even beyond where the mountains are nothing more than hazy, purple curtains. Our world has no boundaries. Our thoughts and dreams and hopes soar beyond the boundaries of our world and, perhaps, that is the very essence of tranquillity.

Dawn on Hawley Lake near Pinetop. David Muench

Rain

It just happened to be one of those years—the year it rained. Rainy years have been few and far between in this arid land of ours, but the welcome rains came last winter and spring...

People who live in wetter areas of our blessed land, who might receive seven or eight inches of rain in a single day, might not be impressed by our boastful figures, but when your average rainfall is six inches a year (a figure that hasn't been reached in years), an over-average is something to be very happy about.

Rain and the miracle of spring brought life to the desert land and millions, maybe billions, of wild flowers raised their colorful heads in grateful salute...Rain sure can pretty up the land...

Folks can get mighty philosophical about rain. Like the old-timer said, squinting up at the blue, clear sky, "It'll rain! It always has!"

(Left) Tonto Creek below the Mogollon Rim.
(Right) Rustler Park in the Chiricahua Mountains.
(Below) Approaching thunderstorm at Sunset Crater.
Jerry Sieve photos

A soft Sleepiness

You can't always tell by the cool calculations
of the calendar or the bobbing babble of the
thermometer. The testimony of the way-
ward Sun is not always reliable. You awaken
one fine morning and for some indefinable
reason you know summer is just around the
corner. There is a languor in the shadows
and a soft sleepiness in the air that bespeak
summer's approach. There is a drowsiness
in the gossip of the green, green leaves
caressed by the soft, warm breeze. You
know that spring has had her fling and
another season is getting ready to cavort

Cooley Lake in the White Mountains. Jerry Jacka

Canyons Calling

Wherever you go in this land of ours you'll come across canyons. You'll even find them on mountaintops as you will when you visit Chiricahua National Monument in the Chiricahua Mountains in Cochise County. The canyons themselves in this area are bounded by rock formations in every conceivable size and shape, mounded deftly by all the tools of the weather.

Where the hills and the mountains break off into the desert you come upon marvelous canyon formations. Sabino Canyon joins the desert and the mountains in Pima County retaining both the design of desert and mountain, losing nothing but gaining from the two, and remaining a canyon in every detail, truly a scenic spot and delightful to see.

And so it goes in this, the canyon country. You will find big canyons and little ones, each with a personality of its own. Tombstone, Aravaipa, Bloody Tanks, White Horse, Six Shooter, Echo, Cave Creek, White and Red and Black and Green—all canyons as picturesque as their names, to mention a few in the endless list. When the time comes to travel again the exciting trails through our West, and it will come soon, you can seek out canyons for yourself. The canyons and the country will be here. The canyons are part of the country, and like the country they never change, for they are governed only by the moods of time, wind, and the weather....

(Left) Morning mist in the rocky canyons near Sedona. Steve Bruno
(Right) Ribbon Falls in the Grand Canyon. Jody Forster
(Following panel) Hiking through time in the Grand Canyon. George McCullough

Navajoland

Navajoland is a wonderful island of geology, geography, anthropology, and meteorology, a parcel of landscape unique in these United States. It is a big land, and within its borders resides the largest Indian tribe in the country.

It is mostly high plateau land, in places cruelly carved with deep canyons, in places supporting harsh mesas, and in places there are a few mountain ranges (Navajo Mountain, the Chuskas, the Lukachukais, for instance) whose pine-covered summits extend regally and eternally into the deep blue canopy of sky.

It is not a "pretty" land, but a harshly beautiful land. The gentle greens of gentler lands are not to be found here. The predominant colors are red and orange and burnt yellow, searing splashes of cruel color under the relentless tyranny of the Sun.

Here the capricious wind finds room for its gambolings, turning red cliffs into rolling sand dunes, carving those very cliffs into strange and contorted formations—all evidence of the mighty power of the singing wind.

Navajoland is an arid land, so arid it puzzles the beholder that the patient Navajos can find enough fodder to support their grazing herds of sheep. And when the storms come they do so with such fury one marvels the red earth itself can endure such onslaughts.

In this land of distance and elusive horizons live the Navajos, whose love of their land is a religion. They are inured to the vagaries of the elements. They accept the wind, the Sun, the lack of rain, all the tempestuous quirks of time and weather—with stoic resignation, for all such things are their gods' will.

They find their land good. It was good when they moved into it hundreds of years ago. It is good today....

Navajo shepherds in Monument Valley.
Herb and Dorothy McLaughlin

Patient Ones

The adjective that best describes the people who live in that vast expanse of Sun, sand, and silence that we know as the land of the Hopi and Navajo Indians is "patience."

Time has neither beginning nor end for them. It is not a few days of light squeezed in between walls of darkness, hurried moments of consciousness like a fever to take possession of one and fill one's head with torment. Time, for them, is all the yesterdays, all the todays, all the tomorrows that flow like a great river from nowhere to everywhere and return. There is no stopping the river. It flows on and on. And with it flow the tears, hopes, joys, and heartaches that are the fabric of living woven into life for we are part of the river, its course is our journey.

Theirs is the patience borne from that wisdom. In their land of little rain, they wait for the rain, and when the rain does not come there is no end to waiting. Waiting is the lot of humankind. If it does not rain today, it will surely rain tomorrow.

The wind, the Sun, the harsh land are part of their destiny. It is foolish to fret with the elements that form the very sinews of existence. The stern elements of life have their compensation. Without them how could one enjoy the stars at night, the exultation of morning, the soaring sense of being a part of the free land itself?

All things have come to them, and all things have passed. The Navajo silversmith sits by the hour pounding his dreams into metal. It does not matter how long he sits there. In the end there will be beauty. The Hopi whittles away at a stick and slowly from his hands comes a little Kachina doll, and that, too, is beauty.

All life is beautiful when from the great wisdom of life you learn patience....

(Right) Ear of the Wind arch in Monument Valley. James Tallon
(Far right) Claret cup cactus blooms. Tom Till

(Left) Sunset over Willcox Playa.
Josef Muench
(Below) Sulphur Spring Valley
in southeastern Arizona.
David Muench
(Right, below) Sunrise over
the Pinaleño Mountains near
Safford. Jerry Sieve

Skies and Grass

The words of the old refrain have been with us since childhood, and too often, like the words of a familiar prayer, a great hymn, or an intimate ballad, they lose their meaning by being sung and resung, told and retold.

America...O beautiful for spacious skies... Old words, old tune, yet brave new words, brave new tune.

These are our skies, the skies of Arizona, one of the precious things about this big land of mountains and desert. These are the skies that cloak distant horizons, a fitting backdrop for such regal settings. There is strength in our skies and bigness and promise and might. There is poetry, too, and music, and they have something sacred about them, like religion. There are the kind of skies that lift men's eyes, the kind of skies you should look at with your soul...

The skies of our land are ever-changing, yet changeless. Each day brings a new, bright sky, with new patterns in sunlight and clouds, enhanced by varying shades of blue. These are skies that make a proper canopy over a new land, where only yesterday, it seems, new trails were cut, new lands were found by the adventuresome people searching the new horizons.

Grass, not gold, is the basis of empire. Civilizations have perished because of the lack of it and the neglect of it. Nations have become great because of an abundance of it. It is one of God's greatest gifts to man, least appreciated, most abused. It is the supreme triumph of the chemistry of soil, rain, Sun.

Grass is Earth's natural cover. When this panoply disappears, the Good Earth is exposed to the ravages of wind and rain. The soil becomes lifeless, and all life supported by the soil perishes. Grass for our people has meant sorrow, despair, exultation. Grass is triumph and tragedy.

A sea of grass is beauty and utility. A million delicate roots clutching the soil, holding it in place, nurturing it! A million blades of grass bespeaking a bountiful land, the well-being of the people who are of the land....

Desert Storm

There is anger in the storm. There is anger in the howling wind, and anger, too, in sonorous and sinister rolls of thunder as if some mad gods were kicking tin cans across the sky. The cruel lightning flashes are like strokes of great swords held by madder gods flailing each other to settle their lordly quarrels. Ever since the beginning of time humankind has been afraid of the storm. Our distant uncles and their kinfolks sat huddled and shivering in their caves when outside the elements were cutting capers and clawing at the Earth. They attributed the storm to the fury of supernatural beings and shivered all the more. They defied the forces of the sky and weather, and today simpler peoples do the same thing, with the sun the beneficial god and inclement weather signs of disapprobation of lesser and more perverse gods holding court with the Sun. We understand the storm now, but we cannot control it....

There is drama in the storm. Sky and Earth meet and are one, and the beholder, if he has a comfortable seat, is afforded

divine entertainment. This is especially true in our western country where the sky is endless and the land stretches on and on. The faraway mountain ranges, seen as bright purple through the rarified atmosphere, turn darker as the clouds form over them and cloud shadows blot out the sun. The sky gets darker and darker as if the lights were being dimmed on the stage, there is lightning like probings of strong spotlights, thunder the sound of drums, and a curtain of rain, slanting with the wind, joining the sky and Earth so that you cannot tell where one begins and the other leaves off....

There is beauty in the storm. The great thunderheads of summer have a massiveness and a grandeur never found in other cloud formations. They form, they pour their moisture to the Earth, and then they break up and scatter....

Evening thunderstorm over Tucson.
Robert Campbell
(Following panel) Storm clouds reaching skyward over Mesa. Bruce Vanderhaar

Grand Canyon Storm

The clouds show the way of the wind. There are no clouds and no wind as a long summer day begins at Grand Canyon. The sky is dark blue overhead, light blue, almost white, at the horizon as if there was not enough blue to go around. It is a big sky, this sky that covers the Canyon. The shadows in the Canyon are long and cool, crazy shaped shadows as if the turrets and pinnacles that cast them are stretching and twisting in grotesque postures after a night's repose. Giants with sleep and dreams in their eyes....

Mid-morning! The Sun rides his chariot higher into the sky. Shadows grow shorter. The hot breath of the Sun weakens the color in sky and Earth. The river digging in the bottom of the Canyon becomes a streak of glinting silver...

The four-o'clock sky over the Canyon is a dark, brooding sky, heavy with moisture. The fitful gusts of wind will shake the patient cedars on the rim and kick up dust along the trails that crawl down steep rock walls. Flashes of lightning leap out of the dark sky. The cloud gods are flailing the Earth with angry whips. Thunder echoes in the depths of the Canyon.

Then out in the Canyon it begins to rain. Patches here and there, moving about, curtains of water spilling out of the sky, and as you watch you cannot see where Earth begins and the dark sky ends. Lightning continues the mad dance, and the thunder is a great wave of noise flooding the Canyon. The Sun, defiant of the storm, breaks through the clouded sky and, to show what a clever fellow he is, hangs a rainbow out in the Canyon for all the world to see.

The storm is short-lived. The Sun parts the clouds and the rain stops. The dark sky breaks up in little pieces and each little piece becomes a white cloud and the white clouds hitch a ride with the wind and go tumbling along to other places. The newly-washed Canyon is clean and bright after the rain. The Sun seems to be brighter than ever and then with a triumphant smile and satisfied with a good day's work he decides to call it a day. Before he leaves, he fills the Canyon with gold that gradually turns to deep purple. The evening sky is clear and studded with bright, twinkling gems called stars and a summer day and a summer storm end at Grand Canyon.

Storm in the Grand Canyon. Kathleen Norris Cook

(Above) Houseboating in Iceberg Canyon, Lake Mead.
James Tallon
(Right) Evening solitude on Lake Mohave.
J. Peter Mortimer

Water and the Thirsty Land

I am the thirsty land. Aeons ago I was covered by ancient seas, knew the sad, rhythmic comings and goings of the restless tides. Then the seas subsided, and I became a morass of mud and green, slimy things. I knew the clump-clump of large, ungainly beasts with unpronounceable names, and they were happy wallowing in my mud. The centuries passed unhurriedly—tens of thousands of centuries, and as the centuries passed, I and the Earth changed. The rains became scarcer and scarcer, and I and all living things I supported were left to the mercy of the relentless Sun. The Sun was a demanding dictator. Conform to the ways of the Sun or perish. There was no alternative. And so all living things that were part of me conformed to the dictates of the Sun. Thus it is that I am as I am, the thirsty land, nuturing a form of plant and animal life adapted to the ways of the Sun, strange in many respects, but sturdy enough to flourish in an area of little rain. The will to live on the part of all living things that are part of me is remarkable to behold. Leaves turned to spines, diurnal habits changed to nocturnal habits, and countless other wiles and tricks to fill a library of books. What could be more astonishing than my wild flowers that will be dormant for as long as a decade or so because the rains did not come and then when rains come turn me into a gorgeous garden? Come to me and study my ways, and leave a wiser man.

Our Southwest

The name "Southwest" could start a lot of arguments. It is conceivable that residents of Chickasha or Big Cabin, Oklahoma, could consider themselves true Southwesterners or that folks living in Dallas, Sugar Land, Big Spring, Muleshoe, Mesquite or Sherman, Texas, would claim they were deep in the heart of the Southwest. It is further conceivable that a geographer would scoff at such claims and by merely pointing to a map say the true Southwest is Southern California, but, to us, that doesn't seem to ring a bell. Maybe the "Southwest" is more a state of mind than an explicit geographical fact.

Our Southwest is a large piece of landscape of which Arizona is the center and which would encompass strips of our neighboring states— California, Nevada, Utah, Southwestern Colorado, New Mexico and, for good measure, our neighbor to the south, Sonora, Mexico.

Our Southwest is hemmed in between the Coastal range on the west and the high Rockies on the east. It is a generally barren, arid, empty land, harsh in some ways, fantastically colorful in others, a land that seems to be swallowed in distance, canopied with the endless blue of endless skies in which seasonal storms drift in to add a spice of contrast and change, giving by their presence respite from what can become a monotonous Sun.

Our Southwest, as we describe it, is by far the most scenic area in these United States. It takes in within its boundaries numerous national parks, and many national monuments, national recreational areas, national historical shrines, state parks, national forests, and Indian reservations. It is difficult to keep a count of all that have been set aside for our pleasure and the pleasure of future generations.

One of the oldest inhabited parts of our country, Our Southwest is essentially the least inhabited. By square mile count, our population is so small the land could almost be called empty, but there are enough folks around so that one does not lack for neighbors.

That's how we describe Our Southwest.

Saguaro Lake, one of four major lakes on the Salt River east of Phoenix. James Tallon

A Dam & a Lake

First there was the Earth, a sodden mudball Divinely created.... Then the mud hardened, and eventually crevices were formed on Earth's obdurate crust, and little trickles of water began to dig the crevices deeper and deeper. One of these crevices became known as Glen Canyon, and the trickle of water that formed it became known as the Colorado, one of the great rivers of America.

Glen Canyon! Remote, lonely, and hauntingly beautiful, was known to ancient people, to the Navajos, to a few early-day explorers, and then in modern times to a few hardy and adventuresome river enthusiasts forever seeking the lonely and out-of-the-way places. The mighty river flowed on and on through the silent Canyon.

Then to harness the strength of the river, a dam was built....

Comes Autumn: the Gentle, Welcome Intruder...

But if I'd ever leave you,
It couldn't be in autumn...

Autumn along Oak Creek, Steve Bruno

*A*utumn. You will find autumn in the mountains along the road through the aspen. The leaves, a few weeks ago so green and shiny and sparkling in the sunlight, have turned to yellow, gold, red, and brown. For the touch of autumn is a magic touch, and autumn is in the air. The wind tugs at the leaves. They fall to the ground to dance before the wind, and they are crisp and crunchy underfoot. Soon all the leaves will be gone from the aspen, and the branches, so white and delicate, will hum a different tune to the music of the wind.

All the flowers are gone now...insects, whose voices were raised to summer's song are gone, too. Summer is over, and it is time to rest. The colors have faded from Earth's covering; a warmer carpet has been spread, a thick brown carpet deep enough and warm enough to keep out the cold of winter.

The days of autumn are shorter, and they hurry along as if they had more important business elsewhere. There is frost on the ground in the morning, and the air has a bite and a nip. Night falls swiftly, and there is not that lingering twilight that marks the days of summer. The stars have a steely look, as if they, too, felt the season's change.

Yet not even spring is more beautiful in the mountains than autumn. The colors of the leaves turning before autumn's touch are extravagantly rich, a profusion of gold coin, turning to more solemn tones, flung over the land. Against the color of the turning leaves, the green of the pine and spruce stand out, and even the blue of the sky takes on a depth and character it does not possess at any other time during the year.

Autumn brings a hush to the mountain world, as if all the world were tensed and waiting. The gossipy, chattering birds have taken their gossip and chatter to other places. What you hear is the sound of crispy brown leaves dancing before the wind.

(Right) Log watering trough in the White Mountains. Jerry Jacka
(Below) Detail of aspen leaves. Kathleen Norris Cook

Mountain Music

There is persuasion in the invitation of the cool, green silence of the mountains while summer's heat still envelops the lowlands. In just a couple of whiles from the desert one can find streams, lakes, meadows, and the eternal music of the pines telling their age-old secrets to the wind.

Hannagan Meadow along the Coronado Trail.
Jerry Jacka

September

September's arrival on the Arizona calendar is always an auspicious one. The month heralds the coming of autumn and finds summer beginning to pack up the more dazzling items of her wardrobe. Out here in Arizona the changing of the seasons is not something that takes place overnight but is a gradual, almost imperceptible process, not harsh or impatient, but gentle and calm. So summer is still with us in September, you understand, but autumn is in the air. September's weather is just about perfect.

For the traveler, September and October are perfect travel months. All Arizona beckons, and it would be hard to find two months more perfect for the adventurer to follow the open road. You will like September, in our land.

(Right) Frosty dawn greets the ghost town of Jerome.
Willard Clay
(Below) Mule deer and ground squirrel get ready for winter. James Tallon photos

The Mellow Month

If you are like us, you love ice cream, fried chicken, and October. October is a dreamy month, a mellow month, when the summer Sun has been toned down in its intensity, and the rather frigid blasts of winter, not too far over the horizon, have not arrived to force one to turn on the heating system. October is a month one doesn't have to hide from. The month beckons one to follow the sorceress trail to the highland and the woodland where October's beauty proclaims old Mother Nature at her colorful best.

(Above) Enjoying the last warm days of autumn.
Tom Canby
(Left) Country road through an aspen glade near
Flagstaff. Dick Dietrich

October

October in Arizona has a split personality. On the desert, the weather is warm and mild, as if summer had taken a liking to the place and was very reluctant to leave. In the higher country, however, it is definitely autumn. The leaves are turning, and there is a chill in the air both morning and evening.

(Left and below) Maple trees in Maple Canyon, Chiricahua Mountains. Willard Clay photos
(Right) An old cabin nestles in an autumn forest. Dick Canby

So the Seasons Change

Out of the north and across the wide expanse comes autumn, the gentle, welcome intruder, dispelling the last caress of summer, carefree truant in the carefree land. The leaves have lost their bright green, turning to brown, orange, red, yellow, touched by the season's enchantment. So gradual and casual is the change in dress in these proud high mountain dwellers that it seems as if they hardly change at all—yet one day the change is complete, and the leaves fall dry and brown and crisp to the ground....They came from the Earth, and they return to the Earth, so completing their life's span...and a life well-spent.

Autumn is a new world. The Sublime Stagehand has shifted the scenery. The seasons change. It is time to think long thoughts of the high mountains and aspen groves and the leaves brown and dry and crisp hurrying along the ground before the wind from the north that autumn brings....

Along the road to Escudilla Mountain near Alpine.
Jerry Jacka

November

Of all the months in the year, November in
Arizona can lay claim to being the most
beautiful. Autumn is still about in the mountains
with warm days and chilly nights. The heat of
summer has gone from the Earth, where the
serenity of evening skies and placid days foretell
the winter season, when all the world, it seems,
comes knocking at our door. Welcome stranger!

Autumn reflections on the Mogollon Rim. Jerry Jacka

Heart of the Forest

A man, for his own well-being, for peace of mind, and for the good of his immortal soul, should spend a couple of weeks each year deep in the heart of the forest. There the soft murmur of the breeze in the pines, the most beautiful music on earth, will calm jumpy nerves, and a few hours a day tramping along a trout stream, will not only whet the appetite but will clear the cobwebs from the mind.

(Left) Colorful maples in West Fork of Oak Creek. Bob Clemenz
(Below) Autumn leaves in the Kaibab Forest on the Grand Canyon's North Rim. Josef Muench

We take you to a forest...and we probe with you into the many things, large and small, that compose one of Nature's most impressive creations. A leisurely forest stroll, we assure you, can not only be fun but very revealing.

In the Kaibab National Forest north of Grand Canyon...is a very special fellow, the Kaibab squirrel. When you travel a highway from Jacob Lake to the Canyon's North Rim, please take a couple of hours off and go wandering off into a pine grove. Your wandering can be very rewarding. You might, if you are patient and observant enough, meet his honor, the Kaibab squirrel. He's unique. There's not another like him on Earth.

Autumn Leaves

Autumn is that period of the year that falls between summer and winter. The season features such wonderful nonsense as school, football, little boys reluctantly raking leaves, pumpkins, Halloween, headliners back on the radio and television programs, turkeys, Thanksgiving, the clank of radiators and the repair of furnaces...thoughts of Christmas gifts, pumpkin pie and cranberry sauce, fireplaces, evening slippers, the comforting pipe, and—oh, yes!—comely young ladies trying to make evening gowns fit in such a way so summer tans, laboriously acquired, won't show in the wrong places.

Autumn is the season, first and foremost, when we glorify leaves—just plain, old leaves.... In the spring, we are more concerned with blooms and blossoms. Our world in autumn is a world of leaves. The season makes us leaf conscious. There is no greater miracle than a leaf...a large cottonwood would probably have as many as 80,000....

Look twice, think twice, when you meet autumn on a mountainside. There is sorcery in the season.

The magic of life in an autumn forest. (Left) Tree frog.
Peter Kresan
(Right) A new tree amid a colorful summer past.
Dick Canby photos

Winds and Mummies

Canyon de Chelly and its famous tributary Canyon del Muerto rise in the Chuska Mountains that form in part the northeastern boundary of Arizona. The canyons cleave through red and yellow and gray sandstone that towers in sheer cliffs and pinnacles and domes hundreds of feet above narrow sandy floors. The twin gorges, characterized by "cliff dwellings like mud-daubers nests, and foot holes in solid rock, leading mysteriously upward," are on the Navajo Indian Reservation and are included in the Canyon de Chelly National Monument....

Here, guarded by overhanging cliffs, protected from decay by dry Arizona air, are found ruined houses, graves, mortuary offerings, and refuse middens; veritable galleries of pictographs carved on cliff rocks; subterranean ceremonial chambers; turquoise pendants with intricate mosaic designs...finely woven baskets; stone-tipped lances...mummies who whisper the story of a succession of cultures....

Autumn comes to Canyon de Chelly National Monument. David Muench

Nature's Paint

Nowhere on Earth's surface does Nature paint with more vivid colors, erect and mould on a more grandiose scale than in our Southwest. To describe the scenic wonders of this area would be a puny gesture. How can mortals with their grimy ink pots catch the mood and the grandeur and the rugged nobility of time's ageless carvings? Can cold words on cold paper, guided by a human's narrow vision and narrower intellect, portray the warmth, the depth, the all-encompassing, the all-powerful message written in stone by the mad winds, the riotous storms, and changing seasons of the tired centuries, punctuated by the sardonic laughter of a bright Sun, whose aeons are but a fleeting paragraph scrawled in the dust?

We can only point to these temples of time and the river in awe and reverent silence. How diaphanous and evanescent, how unimportant the events of our life and times, when we stand before these pillars of forever! The headlines of our day fade into nothing when viewed in surroundings which bear in bold outline a million years of history's story. It is good for the soul to pause occasionally and give heed to these sermons in colored stone, listen to the gentle symphonies of wind mellowed by the blue sky and bright sunshine, or shiver in the wild cacophony of storm in these cathedrals of agelessness.

How amusing it must be to Nature, and her faithful servants, time and the weather, to view man's monument to tomorrow and his tribute to the past and present on either side of this continent! We can imagine the raucous laughter and high mirth as Nature views these piles of glass, iron, and concrete. "I have builded and destroyed for fifty million years. I will build and destroy long after your puny fairs and expositions have vanished into dust and forgetfulness. Only I can tell of past; only I build for tomorrow."

Autumn gold in Canyon del Muerto. Wayne Davis

Pintail ducks flush in morning light. James Tallon

May the Song of Birds Be with Us Always...

Without the song of birds our battered old planet would be very dull indeed!

Without the color of birds our tired old planet would be less colorful and considerably drabber than it is now!

A bird is a creature of God, perhaps one of His most delicate and exquisite creations. Those bumbling old bipeds, Homo sapiens, who think they're the Lords of all creation... can't do what a bird can do—they can't fly. At least they can't without the use of mechanical props, gasoline, aerodynamics, and jet fuel. Ha! Those old vainglorious stumble-bums still have a lot to learn from birds...we dedicate these pages with warmest affection to bird lovers everywhere and especially to those members of the National Audubon Society....

The Philosophic Saguaro

The nights are cool in the desert, and the mornings are crisp and clear. November has caressed the mountains with frosty fingers, and the aspen leaves, like flakes of burnished gold, have carpeted the ground, awaiting winter's covering of snow.

The desert becomes alive in November, peopled by travelers from afar who seek the rest and the peace and contentment to be found there. The desert roads and desert trails resound again with the happy voices of people engaged in the delightful occupation of killing time in a place where time stands still. There is no hurry in the desert. The philosophic saguaro, ageless and mute, gives eloquent testimony to the utter uselessness of the modern individual's fuss and furor. Truly the person beset with the problems of a too transient existence and a too complicated world can learn lessons on the Arizona desert that will never be learned in books.

The November Sun on the desert, as it is throughout the fall and winter months here in Arizona, is warm and restful and invigorating. The desert, clothed in this garb of sunshine— its atmosphere the concoction of the very gods themselves—becomes a religion that will stay with a person forever....

Wintry clouds settle onto the foothills of Sabino Canyon near Tucson.
Willard Clay

Where the Lions Dwell

The hills and mountains of Arizona are apparitions on the horizon—jagged and saw-toothed. The Sun and clouds play a symphony of color on them, and at night, starlit and eerie, they loom in the moonlight, strange and far-away, dim in distance and mystery.

Sunrise over the hills and mountains of Arizona is a sight to behold. In the east, the rising Sun builds a halo of soft gold, as if gentle, unseen fingers were enveloping the crests with burnished cloth. The color becomes more intense as the fire god rises in the heavens, and soon the east is aflame, and the hills and mountains are aglow with fire—leaping fire of red and living gold.

Then the fires fade into cold purple-blue embers as morning shadows cling to the outline, and soon the hills and mountains are cold and clear in the bright Sun, and above is the clear blue sky with an errant white cloud loitering by, going no place in a hurry, a sleepyhead with dreams of yestereve still lingering.

When the storms come, the sky is black and heavy over the hills and mountains, and the lightning flashes break through the blackness, livid and repellent. After the storm passes, the mountains glisten in the clear sunlight, so bright and clear they seem, that the unwary traveler will think they are only a few miles away, and then they will taunt you in high mirth as they seem to be farther away the longer you travel toward them....

In the evening, the mountains of Arizona wear robes of rose and garnet, ruby and crimson, as the worn old Sun sinks slowly in the west like a tired old man, happy and proud of his pious centuries, going to bed. The million shades of red over the mountains deepen into fantastic purples before night pulls its magic curtain, and the world sleeps.

These are the high rugged mountains where the lions dwell, where come the winds and the storms, and from where on clear days you see new horizons far, far away....

Arizona high country, where the lions dwell.
First snow comes to San Francisco Peaks. Wesley Holden

Arizona's Winter: a Synonym for Sunshine...

*And could I leave you
Running merrily through the snow?*

Winter scene on the range land near Elgin. Willard Clay

When you spend your winter in the Old West you have all of southern and central Arizona to choose from; and much of northern Arizona has that delightful winter climate that beckons.

Winter of snow and cold comes only to our high mountains. Only our loftier peaks and higher elevations wear coats of ermine, and they do so proudly, for theirs is a noble mission. They seem to stand like mighty guardians against the storms that come with winter, and in their strong arms they seize the storms' challenge and struggle ever-victoriously to protect the pleasant valleys and the desert below.

Here is the snowdrift on the mountainside, whose silence is broken by the breaking of a snow-heavy twig on the pine tree or the happy shout of a figure on skies gliding rhythmically through the alabaster of snow and sunlight.

Down below, but an hour or so away, is that glorious admixture of winter, spring, summer, and along a trail rides a couple of carefree people whose wide hats shade their faces from the Sun, their horses munching occasional patches of grass, their faces reflecting the joyousness of their surroundings and the exhilaration of bright, sun-drenched out-of-doors in the Old West.

From the high mountains in morning comes the zestful freshness in the air, invigorating and enlivening to the valleys and desert below. This is the kind of air one would like to bottle and have for all time; for no other air on Earth is quite like it. It is the desert and the mountains and the sky and sunlight all mixed up, and its label is "Arizona."

Arizona cattle country between Flagstaff and Winslow. Jerry Jacka
(Right) Southern Arizona visitors enjoy a trail ride on a wintry afternoon. J. Peter Mortimer
(Right, below) Home for the holidays. Val Stannard

A bit of Arctic

The business of winter sets in early in the northern part of this land, and with winter comes the snow, hard and bright and clean. 'Way up in the San Francisco Peaks near Flagstaff you might find snow any time after the first day of November. And sometimes it remains on the rocky slopes of the mountain until July. But this is just a little bit of the Arctic in a land where summer and spring are mostly in season. In these mountains and in the higher elevations where snow comes early and is piled deep, people with skis seek the snow and plunge down mountainsides on the wings of winter. And to these people snow is sport.

Snow is many things to many people in this land, where, to very, very few, snow is a hardship.

Snow is a fearful thing to many people in colder climes, with its attendant evil companions: cold and sleet and freezing weather. But here winter's white garment loses its terror. It becomes something different for nearly every person who lives in or near it.

Lonesome winter scene south of Flagstaff. Jerry Jacka

Winter Serenade

Night was a whirling mass of darkness, with savage voice and with savage fingers clawing at the mountain. There were no stars. Creatures of the night eschewed familiar paths and haunts to wisely remain warm and secure in sequestered places. There was only the wind and the voice of the night. The trees were bent wraiths, flinching before the anger of the wind.

The storm was on a high lonesome on the lonely mountainside.

Far below, feeble lights flickering in the darkness revealed the presence of people. Houses were barred against the storm. The wind rattled loose gates and window shutters, raging to be denied the warmth within the houses. The broad highway skirting the base of the mountain, with a dark pathway in the night over which an occasional automobile cautiously picked its way. Not a pleasant night to be traveling about in, but fate and destiny decree not all God's creatures shall be warm and secure on cold winter nights.

By morning the storm had blown itself away. There were no clouds, only a sky of blue ice. There was no wind on the mountainside, only silence of a white winter world broken every now and then by the crackling of a limb weighed down with snow. Mountain animals ventured forth from their sequestered places leaving marks in the snow where they walked.

The sunshine straining through the cold, crisp air was bright but not warm so early in the morning, and where the light snow caught the sunshine there was the flash of diamonds, gleaming precious jewels flung about with the spendthrift's grace. The trees on the mountainside threw long shadows, but even there light was reflected so that the snow crystals were blue diamonds. Never were the mountains more beautiful, never was the air more clear.

Snowy boughs unburden themselves into Oak Creek.
Suzanne Clemenz

The Many Mansions of Winter

Winter lives in many mansions in Arizona. There is the winter people in more inclement climates expect and are accustomed to—the winter of white silence in high forests; trees bowed with the weight of the ermine robes they wear; the song of the birds stilled; tracks in the snow, furtive signatures left by small creatures in their comings and goings—the only signs that life exists in a dormant, sleeping world....

Snows fall lightly and gently at the Grand Canyon during the winter, and when they do, the effect is beautiful to behold....

In a land where there is so little snow, snow in Arizona is a thing of beauty, that shining white curtain of cleanliness with which winter creates a wonderland. In the mountain regions of our state, snow comes early and lies deep to feed mountain streams in the spring, which in turn bring moisture to the great reservoirs. Farmers who may never see snow owe their crops to it....

Only very rarely does snow come to the desert. An inch or two will fall some stormy night, and the next morning the desert will blink with the new day on whiteness all around. A saguaro will look the world over, startled by the unexpected and will wear a "See, what a bright fellow I am!" expression. No, snow is not for the desert. An hour or two after the storm comes in the night, the snow will begin to fade, apologetic for the intrusion. And in the sunlight the next noon all the snow will be gone from the desert, and dampness and freshness will remain.

(Right) Winter snow patterns on the South Rim of the Grand Canyon. David Muench
(Below) Pack train emerging from the Grand Canyon. Dick Canby
(Following panel) After a stormy night, first light finds the desert foothills near Tucson covered with snow. Joe Carrder

The Year It Snowed

So the storm passed, and the world wore a cloak of white. The morning sun in a clear, cold sky turned snow crystals into glistening jewels. The cold breath of the storm could still be felt, challenging the Sun. It was as if the furnaces of the Sun had lost their fire, for there was no warmth in the bright light of the sunshine. The wind, which accompanied the storm during the night, left marks of its passing on the sculptured mounds and patterns of clean, white snow, a mantle of sparkling ermine which the Earth wore with proud grace and beauty....

There was drama, majesty, and beauty wrought by the big storm that came the year it snowed, the year it snowed real big.

Winter's fury in the red rock country near Sedona.
Tom Canby

Skiers' Paradise

This is the winter that sports enthusiasts, living in lower and warmer elevations of the state, claim as their personal domain. (A visitor would be surprised to see how many sporting goods stores there are in the desert oases cities of Phoenix and Tucson, for instance, which do a thriving business catering to winter sports needs and whims of Arizonans.) This, too, is the winter that meteorologists and hydrologists study with intense concern because snow in the mountains means spring runoffs, spring runoffs mean water for thirsty lands, and water for thirsty lands means the good life, the assured life, and well-being for so many in so many ways. Knowing that winter has brought snow to the mountains is pleasant knowledge to those who live in the dry and arid land....

That skiing should flourish in a state not ordinarily associated with snow is merely another of those tantalizing contrasts that are to be found here. Visitors to the Sun country can loll about an orange grove in the morning and by noon hurtle a mountainside on a pair of skis. This is probably the only place on Earth where you can have your cake and eat it too....

Cross-country skiing near northern Arizona's Snow Bowl.
Tom Bean

Beyond Where the Roads End

And what, you may ask, is a wilderness area? Well, according to Webster, a wilderness is a "tract of land, or a region, whether a forest or a wide, barren plain, uncultivated and uninhabited by human beings; a wild waste...an area of national forest land set aside by the government for preservation of natural conditions, either for scientific or recreational purposes."

Now we are getting someplace. Our wilderness areas (nine in number) are portions of our seven national forests set aside and protected by the U.S. Forest Service to remain for all time as close as possible to what they were when the Good Lord first made them. Technically we have wilderness, wild and primitive areas,

according to size, but for our purpose "wilderness area" will suffice.

They begin beyond where the roads end. The only sign of man ever passing their way are a few trails for the convenience of the hiker or the person riding a horse. No roads, no automobiles, no Jeeps, no motorcycles, no scooters, nothing mechanized. Here, in these isolated areas, one can at last be free from the odor of carbon monoxide. Fresh air! It's wonderful!

We owe a lot to the Forest Service for setting up such areas for us to enjoy, places where we can be by ourselves if we wish. The debt...for these wilderness areas will be even greater for the generations to come....

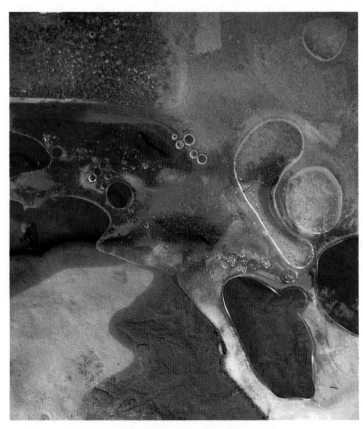

(Left) Silent winter symphony in blue and white. George McCullough
(Right) The Coconino National Forest in winter dress. George McCullough
(Below) Nature's artwork in ice. Tom Canby

Children of Nature

In the Navajo hogan, as the storm passed, all was secure and warm, the family sleeping serenely in their beds of sheepskins and heavy, woolen blankets. All night the coals of the fire glowed in friendly comfort, giving warmth against the cold of night.

When the first rays of the Sun appeared above the horizon, the Navajo father went out to greet the new day. The world that greeted him was a world of winter white, winter bright, the Sun turning the newly fallen snow into a carpet of glistening diamonds. His sheep were huddled together in mutual warmth against the cold. The Navajo found his world good.

On his return to the hogan, he told the Navajo mother, who was busy with the morning meal, "Last night the snow came!" She answered, "That is good! When the snow comes in winter, the grass will come in the spring, and the sheep will grow big, fat and healthy."

The high, barren plateau regions...here live the Navajos, with the weather—good, bad, but never indifferent—their constant companion. They are children of Nature. Nature in many ways has moulded them as it has moulded the land in which they live. They accept the buffets of wind and storm and Sun stoically. Bad weather—as well as good weather—is decreed by their gods. Their respect for the weather is shown in the names they give the months of the year.

December, in Navajo, is "Nitch'l Tson," The Month of Increasing Cold and Wind. January is "Yas Nilt'ees," The Month of Crusting or Icing of Snow; and February is "Atsa Bujaazh," The Month of the Young Eagles Hatching. Names of beauty that fit.

Navajo hogan in winter, Chuska Mountains background.
David Muench
(Following panel) Wintery contrast between the desert and 7645 foot high Four Peaks northeast of Phoenix.
Jerry Jacka

Bright Sun Shining

It is a long journey of some 92,956,000 miles, the mean distance from the Sun to the planet on which we live, but the sunbeam making the trip does so in 498.6 seconds, slightly more than eight minutes. Such a long journey in such a short time could be described as traveling at a very rapid rate, a description that would be the crassest understatement ever understated. Our little sunbeam, with countless other sunbeams just going along for the ride forming light, travels at a clip of 186,282 miles per second, an almost incomprehensible speed to those who were once dumbfounded to learn a daredevil by the name of Barney Oldfield went whizzing along in his gasoline buggy at the fantastic speed of sixty miles per hour. Sound itself is a slowpoke (about 1087 feet per second in dry air at 32 degrees Fahrenheit) compared to light, but in the final analysis, it is not the speed of our little sunbeam that counts (however astonishing!), or the life it brings, but the beauty it creates for all of us.

Our little sunbeam, born in the fiery, raging, inner furnaces of the Sun (25,000,000 degrees Fahrenheit) starts out life in the form of deadly and destructive gamma rays, boiling and roiling and battering its way outward.

It passes through gaseous nuclear bang-ups and collisions, turning itself into X-rays and ultraviolet light, penetrating the Sun's surface photosphere and chromosphere and outer corona from which it finally takes off on its own as visible light and invisible radiation. It is an infinitesimal part of the total energy emitted by the Sun that finds itself on its way to Earth.

Our little sunbeam and its...companions serve many purposes at journey's end, one of which is the contribution of scientific knowledge it makes on its arrival at Kitt Peak Observatory, elevation 6875 feet, located in the desert Papagoland near Tucson. Here the most modern instrument for solar study ever devised by man is ready for its arrival....

But at journey's end, our little sunbeam serves another purpose: it vanquishes night, makes the corn green and the flowers bloom, enriches man's mind and soul with the beauty of a rainbow or a sunset, or shimmering through aspen leaves. Without our little sunbeam, our world would be dull, dark, and ugly, indeed....

(Below and Right) Domes of the Kitt Peak National Observatory reflect sunset glow and rise above a winter morning fog. Gary Ladd Photos

The Beautiful Season

Many, many, many years ago—just yesterday, in fact—the firm light of a bright new star guided three wise and kindly men through another and faraway desert seeking a newborn in a simple manger. Since then, through the placid and turbulent centuries, during this season the stars shine with greater warmth, greetings between friends are more friendly, man is more considerate and thoughtful of the needs and afflictions of man.

During this season we think not only of ourselves. More so than at any other time of the year those of well-being think of others, the selfish are less selfish, the miser less a miser. Our loved ones, near and far, are closer to us than before, the blessings we enjoy and our happiness we wish to share with those less favored.

The light that illuminated the newborn in that simple manger so many, many, many years ago shines more brightly today. The centuries proclaim the wisdom of His message of peace on Earth and of human righteousness and decency.

Let the bells ring out the message of the season. Never do bells sound so inspiring. Let voices be raised in the season's songs, the grandest songs ever sung on Earth.

This is Yule. This is the Beautiful Season.

(Right) A giant saguaro silhouetted against an Arizona sunset. Jerry Jacka
(Below) Mission San Xavier del Bac, Tucson. Willard Clay
(Following panel) Organ Pipe Cactus National Monument. Jody Forster

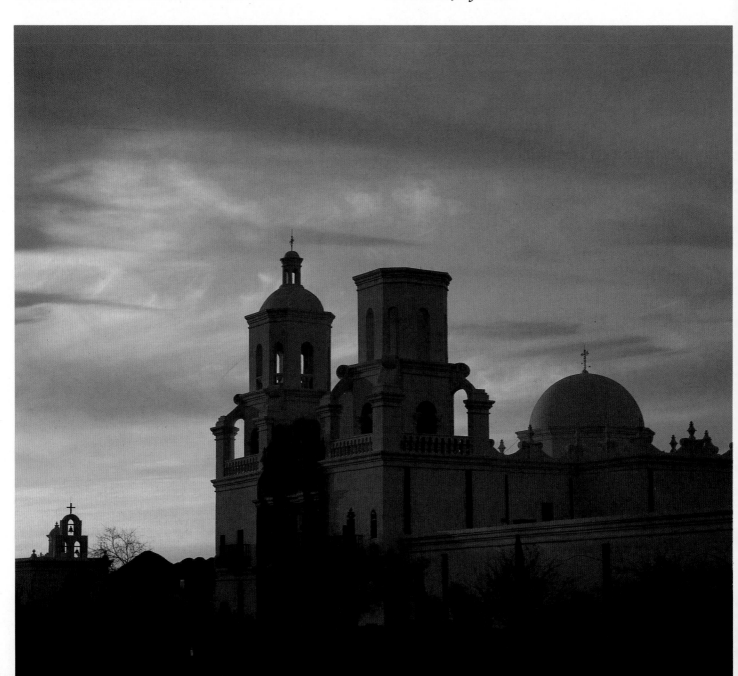

Look to the Skies

Look to the skies for beauty, for rest, for
inspiration and quiet reverie. Look to the skies
for those precious moments in your life when
your mind and heart soar to higher and finer
things, and you lift your eyes from the mundane.
All the world is a cathedral and the sky the
sacred dome of Heaven that covers it. Look to
the skies, then, for guidance, for comfort, for
understanding. Here is nourishment for the
soul, pinched by the confinements and the
harassments of everyday living. This is the way
God made the world, and the sky is always with
us. It is our fault that we look down and follow
little footsteps in the dust. And if all we get is
dust in our eyes only we are to blame. Behold
the skies! Course of the Sun and pathway of
the Moon and clouds! Behold the skies!

Sonoran Desert sunset. Alan Benoit

Spring Brings God's Blossoms...

If ever I would leave you,
How could it be in springtime,

A late snow caps blooms on Hopi peach trees
in northern Arizona. Jerry Jacka

$\mathcal{S}$pring, enchanting sorceress, brings the flowers to the desert and puts the bloom and color in our desert bouquet. The desert is always a thing of beauty, but in spring it primps and poses and takes on a loveliness that to the beholder bespeaks the stroke of some magic wand. No matter how often you see it, our desert bouquet, with its myriad flowers, is a memorable sight....

Those who live in the desert or those whose leisure moments are spent in following its lazy, dusty trails say that generally desert flowers bloom from Washington's Birthday to the Fourth of July. The flowering season will vary with the year but if you seek your bouquet April, May, and June are delightful months for your search. At this time you are sure to find the desert wearing the gayest of corsages.

If you should be lucky enough to wander into the desert during what desert folks call a "wet" spring, then you will see the desert at its best. A green carpet of grass is stretched invitingly before you. Poppies and many other small flowers dance their dance in the sun. In places they are so thick they make up the patterned floor covering that rolls out before you almost as far as you can see. During a "dry" spring, the seeds that hold these flowers lie dormant in the desert soil, holding their charm for more favorable weather.

During a "wet" spring you will discover the cacti vying with each other to produce the largest blossoms in greatest numbers, spendthrifts spending their beauty with lavish recklessness. Rain is the miracle worker in the desert....

Regardless of the whims of the rain gods, the desert always pays fitting tribute to the smiling season. The flowers may not be so numerous, but they are just as exquisite and bewitching, their colors as vivid and luminous, their petals as waxy and delicate, the craftsmanship that formed them just as exacting and elegant.

The aimless roads follow their aimless ways into the desert, inviting you to the purple hills not so far ahead. You who seek will have no trouble finding your desert bouquet this spring. The flowers are there awaiting you....

Spring in Organ Pipe Cactus National Monument.
Kaz Hagiwara

The Days of Spring

Those were the days of spring—the bright Sun in the desert, the warm and friendly Sun, a lazy and languorous Sun popping out of a clear sky, full of blue and punctuated with a lazy cloud or so.

For all people sometime will return to the desert in spring...whatever missions call them to whatever lands and islands beyond the seas....

There is color in the desert in spring and music and the fragrance of a world new and clean and bright, a world redolent with charm and sunshine...a lazy world but a lovely one, and a world of peace....

Spring will miss many of her companions in the desert this year, their destinies having taken them to far places or are keeping them in far places busy with tasks important to their fate and to their nation, far from the desert in spring. But the desert people will return some other spring when peace comes again to the land....

And that spring the desert shut you out from all the world, and soon you felt how removed the world was and how far away the little joys and troubles that people describe as life, how far away was yesterday. In the desert time stands still, as if it, too, in its inexorable march to eternity has found a pleasant place to pause and linger a bit. The hours spin themselves out slowly, and a day stretches on and on for an endless age to blend like soft music with the softer music of a desert evening in spring.

In the desert you leave the world and your own thoughts behind you. The ways of man and his madness and his moneymaking find no accord in such a place. The scheme of the desert is but a pattern for reveries, for self-searching. Here undisclosed depths reveal themselves with startling clarity, and it is good for a man to see into his own soul.

Editor's note: Raymond wrote this as he departed for combat duty in World War II.

Cholla and saguaro cacti on the Sonoran Desert.
David Muench

Desert Moods

The desert has many faces, and it shows a different face to each and every person. The beholder, on meeting the desert for the first time, will find it almost drab in its simplicity but on better acquaintance will find it fascinating in its complexity, moody and mysterious in the varied and forever-changing facets of its personality.

The desert will never be all things to all people. To some it represents a sweeping emptiness of subtle coloring embracing the sky and the purple mountains, the ageless drapery of shadowed rock that forms the horizon. These people find the desert almost an empty void, cameo clear in the bright, light air, tantalizing in its invitation for further exploration.

The desert is a mighty instrument which records all the nuances and subtle changes of weather, sky, Sun, and cloud shadow. That is why desert lovers never find their beloved land a tale of twice-told monotony. In its agelessness, it is vitally youthful. The better you come to know it, the more you learn of its strange and surprising ways, and that is why true desert lovers never tire of it and find other lands dull in comparison....

"You will be rewarded well for whatever efforts, no matter how meager, you expand in my behalf. My secrets are many. No man can know them all, but those I reveal will in some way enrich your life. You will find me full of moods, full of mysteries, strange in all ways, but ever wise in the ways of the Sun. If you approach me with understanding and a loving heart, you will not find me unfriendly. Come with warm welcome, stranger. My treasures are many, and these I will gladly share with you."

*(Right) The saguaro blossom, Arizona's state flower.
Jerry Jacka
(Below) The pineapple cactus in bloom. David Muench*

Spring...Surprise!

Spring...the friendliest word in the language. Of all the seasons spring seems more intimate and delightful than any other. Throughout all the West—from Powder River in Wyoming to the San Pedro and the Gila in Arizona, from the ranges of Cochise County to Montana—spring is an awakening, something akin to a miraculous happening.

If you live to be nine and ninety or if you're only nine or deliciously nineteen, spring comes upon you all of a sudden as a surprise, bringing round-eyed admiration and wonder. Spring doesn't come in like a tiresome neighbor, full of innocent small talk, droning out the tiresome tales. Spring comes gushing in, bubbling and sprightly, full of laughter and merriment, new and full of music, exciting and thrilling....

But spring! Even when you get into the desert in our land, where seasons change so slowly you barely notice the change, you know that spring is here. The air is just a little bit lighter and the Sun has a particular glow. The skies are just a little bit bluer and the clouds a mite whiter and more billowy than at any other time. And then the flowers just seem to have popped up all about you, and they seem to dance in the breeze and shout laughingly, "Surprise! Surprise!"

Prickly pear cactus blossoms. Jerry Jacka

A Wondrous Thing

Life in the desert is a wondrous, miraculous thing, but, perhaps, most wondrous and miraculous of all is the transformation of drab desert land into a veritable flower garden when rains come in winter and early spring. This takes place not by happenstance or haphazard chance but by the careful blending of all Nature's wonderful nurturing tools to give and sustain life. The rains must come at the right time (some years they do not) to stir life's juices in dormant seeds. When dormant seeds have sprouted, hot, searing winds must take their mischief elsewhere (some years, alas, these mischievous winds are too much with us and our anticipated flower display comes to naught).

Ah! But when all things are right what beauty to behold when drab, desert land is transformed into a glorious flower garden under spring's gentle and magic touch. The usually dry, barren land is clothed in a garb of many hues, radiantly beautiful, almost awesome in its flowered splendor.

It doesn't happen every year, but when it does, it's worth waiting and watching for.

(Top) Hedgehog blossom detail. Jerry Jacka
(Left) Saguaro, ocotillo, prickly pear, and hedgehog along the Apache Trail east of Mesa. David Muench

Wild Flower Paradise

"In the wildest Nature, there is only the material of the most cultivated life, and a sort of anticipation of the last result, but a greater refinement already than is ever attained by man."
—Henry David Thoreau

...And that, dear reader, was the key that unlocked the cell in our mind wherein lived the botanist in our lives...to see botany as another vehicle on the road to the Beautiful Explanation of Life.

The Arizona desert is a perfect place to seek the great truths about Nature and especially about wild flowers.

Because of its geographical position, and range of altitude, in which are represented the five basic climate zones of the wild plant kingdom, Arizona is a paradise for almost 40 percent of the more than 12,000 known flowering plants of the world not grown under cultivation. More than 3438 species are known and listed in Kearney & Peebles' *Arizona Flora,* and they represent those of nearly every part of North America. There are still new species to be discovered in remote, and unexplored areas....

1957 was a peak year...so outstanding that more than 250 species were recorded which had not bloomed for 50 years prior. And they haven't been seen since....

In the Great Plan man is no match for Nature and the Great Spirit. At times Nature rebels, and for several years in succession the Great Spirit sends little rain. Then, when least expected, snows and rains recycle the process of life again. Nature never intended for humans to understand her, no more than we should ever understand the story of the Resurrection, and the mystery, miracle and wonder of life itself, whether it be manifest in plant and seed, mother and child, or the cycle of the seasons.

Yes, indeed, there is nothing like a day in a flower-carpeted desert to convince man that everything spiritual and material is born of the Earth, and man is no more important to God than the dormant seed waiting to be born again.

(Right) The bounty of spring near Bartlett Lake northeast of Phoenix.
Jerry Sieve

(Below)...discovering great truths about Nature.
Dick Dietrich

Ho Hum! It's Spring!

You've seen it all before: birds, bees, blue skies, billowy clouds, and blossoms dripping color. Poets sharpen their pencils, but nothing comes off because the season is much too giddy to stay for a sonnet or a couplet. One should write of spring on cold winter nights when howling wind rattles the shutters. One shouldn't do anything in spring, but just loaf, and get outside, and see what a bright, fine world it is.

The cactus wren, Arizona's state bird, lives in the desert country and having been properly introduced, you will find your spring wanderings more eventful.

But ho hum! It's spring! It is afternoon, and · the bright Arizona Sun is coming down like it was poured out of a bucket, soft and inviting. An editor's office is just no place to be on a warm spring afternoon. You look out the window and there is spring beckoning. You look at your typewriter. Good, faithful friend! You're going to have to shift for yourself until tomorrow. It's spring, you know! Ah! Spring! Here we go to see what a bright, fine world it is outside....

"April in Paris," "April in Portugal" are unforgettable, it's true, but nothing turns us on like April in Arizona. In our land it's a time to feel joyful, romantic, and springtime young, for April brings with her the first warm kiss of spring. The flowers appear anew, the birds exalt in song, and that manifestation of renewed hope and new life is evident in each new bud awakening from winter's sleep. The spirit of resurrection is everywhere with us.

(Top to bottom) Arizona's state bird, the cactus wren; western cottontail rabbit; roundtail ground squirrel.
James Tallon photos
(Right) Ocotillo in bloom near the New Water Mountains of western Arizona. Ed Cooper

A Land that Takes Knowing

Our desert can be, to many people, the most forbidding, the harshest, the most uninviting portion of all God's not-so-green acres. It never has been nor ever will be the most comfortable and easiest portion of our planet on which to work, loaf, ruminate, dream, achieve ambitions, or build castles in the sky!

It is not a pretty, pretty wonderland! It is a land that takes knowing!

Now how do you come to know a desert land? Well, it takes living in, a lot of living in, that's how! It is not an easy land to know, as far as that is concerned. It is not a chummy-chummy land that gives its favors with gay frivolity or can be wooed with a careless toss of the head and an empty smile. It's hot, prickly, dry, ugly, repulsive, unkind, dangerous, rocky, totally without rhyme or reason! It is all of that unless you know it well. As we said it takes a lot of knowing, and then the desert is a different story.

A person coming to the desert for the first time from such places as the Pacific Northwest, the Midwest, the New England states or the deep South comes almost as if from another planet. Nothing in that person's experience has prepared him for the strange and arid land, warned him, we might say, of the weird and startlingly fantastic flora, so unlike anything he might have known in other climes, all shaped by the Sun, all equipped with the necessary armor not to defy the Sun but to live and flourish under all the strict impositions of that very Sun itself....These plants, who find themselves so well adapted to desert ways, are *xerophytic,* meaning, literally, the drier it is and the hotter it is the better they love it.

These are the things the visitor should know: The desert itself is of the Sun, and the creatures living therein are ruled by the Sun.

Gila blooms in May throughout Glen Canyon National Recreation Area in northern Arizona. Jeff Gnass (Following panel) Century plants blooming in south-eastern Arizona. Ed Cooper

Desert Trails

They wander into the desert, these desert trails, winding and twisting, lazily stepping aside now for a saguaro, now for a paloverde. Their destination is the desert edge where the foothills roll upward and lose themselves in the bluish haze of the distant mountain range. This winding path will take you to a ranch house in some small canyon in the foothills where a friendly cottonwood shields it from the sun. Another of these lazy desert trails will lead you to a prospector's camp and another to a small mine and another to a cottage in the desert where someone, shielded in the desert's bosom, is regaining lost health.

Each desert trail is an adventure, a glorious adventure into the sunshine and into the peaceful silence of a great outdoor cathedral. Not any place else on Earth can you be more alone, more immersed in your thoughts, more steeped in the beauty of simple Nature....

(Right) Sand verbena decorate a desert road near Yuma.
James Tallon
(Below) Golden blossoms crown the barrel cactus.
Jerry Jacka

Travelog to Spring

If your quest is spring, come to our land. Every highway in the state—east, west, north, south—will carry you to a happy rendezvous....

Spring's modish trademark is everywhere in our land. The Joshua forest to the west and north of Kingman; the Joshua forest to the west of Congress Junction; the great desert stretch between Chandler and Tucson; that wild remote area, the Organ Pipe Cactus National Monument, south of Ajo; Saguaro National Monument, near Tucson; all the countless miles of foothills and low mountains througout the state, half desert and half mountain: here is spring.

Spring in our land is many things. To the lover and student of cacti, it may be a tiny pincushion holding a large blossom, or it may be that intricate creation of Nature called the blossoming saguaro. To the painter it may be the desert landscape and the distant range of purple mountains, the vivid white clouds lazying above those mountains and the crystalline clearness beyond and above the clouds called blue sky. To the poet it may be the droning of the bees in the mesquite blossom, or the music of a clear, cold stream hurrying down from a snow bank of some high mountain. To the motorist spring may be the carpets of gold and blue wild flowers along the highway, and there are many miles of highway and many miles of wild flowers in our land.

To the rancher spring means the thick grass of the desert floor or the hillsides of grass you find in Santa Cruz County and Cochise County. Spring means to many the citrus trees in blossom, and to others dreamy afternoons just sitting in the Sun....

The dams along the Apache Trail...are this year churning full of water that has come boiling down the watershed to record an all-time mark for storage. Roosevelt Dam, a milepost in the history of reclamation, last spring but a mud-hole is filling to overflow capacity this spring.

Yes, it's spring! A happy, generous, colorful, fragrant spring!

(Above) Joshua blossom detail. John Cacheris
(Right) Joshua trees in spring near Kingman. Jerry Sieve

Arizona...an Enchantress!

Arizona! A magic word. Arizona! What visions of grandeur those seven letters conjure. Arizona! A symphony in mad, extravagant colors, shaded with the soft light of the desert in the evening, the purple mountains at twilight, the mauve sky of a rising sun.

Arizona! An enchantress, with rare and precious jewels worn lightly and gaily, like a new dress to the marketplace. An enchantress, whose jewels, sparkling in the bright sunshine, are more valuable than all the wealth of all the kings and kings' men ever to stride the Earth. Arizona! A tantalizing sorceress, whose charms are graciously and generously bestowed upon one and all alike, and yet whose secrets are held in unfathomable depths, ever-mysterious, ever-alluring.

Arizona! An adventure and a challenge, if you please. Stout men and stout hearts have followed her unending trails, climbed her unbending mountains, to bow at last in admiration and adoration. Arizona! Contradictions and contrasts! Arizona! Moods and majesty.

To all men and all women there is a different Arizona. But to all men as to all women there is one overwhelming Arizona—that is Arizona, the land of great beauty, and Arizona, the land of rich, magnificent color.

Arizona!...R.C.

Nowhere in the world is there anything quite like the fragrance of the desert after a fresh spring rain. Saguaro National Monument West. Thomas Ives
(Following panel) Perfect ending for a perfect day. Willard Clay

Summer, autumn, winter, spring...the beauty of Arizona's
scenic seasons at Red Rock Crossing near Sedona. Dick Canby